learning to
ABIDE

by Adriana Lechin

HigherLife Development Services, Inc.,
PO Box 623307, Oviedo, FL 32762
(407) 563-4806, www.ahigherlife.com

Edited by: Lysa McMillan, Esse Johnson

Designed by: Bella Baker Agency

Published 2025
Printed in the United States of America
30 29 28 27 26 25   1 2 3 4 5

ISBN:978-1-964081-29-8 (paperback)
ISBN:978-1-964081-34-2 (eBook)
Library of Congress Case Number: 1-14539380601

John, though our paths of faith may differ, your unwavering support, love, and understanding have been a constant source of strength and inspiration in my life. This book, grounded in my love for Jesus, is a reflection of my journey and the truths that guide me.

Thank you for walking beside me. I am deeply grateful for the love we share. Always praying for you.

ABIDE— (verb) to remain; continue; stay; dwell; reside; to continue in a particular condition, attitude, relationship; to remain steadfast or faithful.

Abide. Abide is not a word we generally use in our everyday communication, but understanding and embracing its meaning is vital for Christ followers. Jesus defines this spiritual way of life in John 15. If we really want to know Him intimately and experience the supernatural, fruitful, and victorious life found only through union with Christ, we must learn to live it. We must abide.

> *"Abide in Me, and I in you. As the branch cannot bear fruit by itself, unless it abides in the vine, neither can you, unless you abide in Me. I am the vine; you are the branches. Whoever abides in Me and I in him, he it is that bears much fruit, for apart from Me you can do nothing.... As the Father has loved Me, so have I loved you. Abide in My love. If you keep My commandments, you will abide in My love, just as I have kept My Father's commandments and abide in His love. These things I have spoken to you, that My joy may be in you, and that your joy may be full."*
>
> *John 15:4–5, 9–11 (ESV)*

A

"As the Father has loved Me, so I have loved you. *Abide* in My love."
—John 15:9 (ESV)

"So Jesus said to the Jews who believed Him, "If you *abide* in My word, you are truly My disciples, and you will know the truth, and the truth will set you free."
—John 8:31-32 (ESV)

"And now, little children, *abide* in Him, so that when He appears we may have confidence and not shrink back at His coming."
—1 John 2:28 (ESV)

INTRODUCTION

Hi, I'm Adriana! Born in Venezuela, my family and I settled in Florida during my pre-teen years. Currently in my early 30s, I am a proud dog mom to my beloved furry companion, Indi. Indi and I found each other in Colombia while I served as a missionary. I'm also an aunt (or "Titi", as my nieces and nephews lovingly call me), which brings me immense joy.

Faith is a very important part of my life. I am a devoted follower of *Jesus Christ*, chosen by God and set apart for His good purpose. I am filled with His Spirit, inspired by His Word, learning more and more about how to *abide* in His Love.

But it wasn't always that way.

For a while I took a spiritual detour. After many years of growing in the faith and serving Jesus, I experienced deep hurt and disappointment, which led me to question everything I believed in. Eventually I moved away from my faith. Looking back, I realize it wasn't entirely Jesus I was walking away from—but the weight of unrealistic expectations I put on others and myself to be perfect. The pressure was overwhelming. Over time, I had become religious and lost sight of the authentic relationship I once had with Christ.

I wish I could say I ran back to Him, but I didn't. I spent years away from Him. Yet, despite my resistance, Jesus didn't give up on me. I let years pass without opening my Bible. I threw away books, memories, and friendships. I remained distant, but His relentless grace never stopped pursuing me. Eventually, the scriptures I once treasured came alive again, dismantling the lies I'd come to believe about myself, others, and God. Thankfully, He didn't throw my sin in my face, but rather called me in closer. He called me to abide in Him. It was the truth of God's Word that released me from fear and unbelief — and in turn I finally understood what it meant to fully surrender my life to Jesus, my dearest Friend.

This journey of departure and devotion has profoundly shaped my perspective on the Word of God and its transformative power. The Word of God has moved me to share my experience in the form of this journal. For those seeking a deeper spiritual connection with Jesus, I pray this journal will offer inspiration, encouragement, and spiritual guidance.

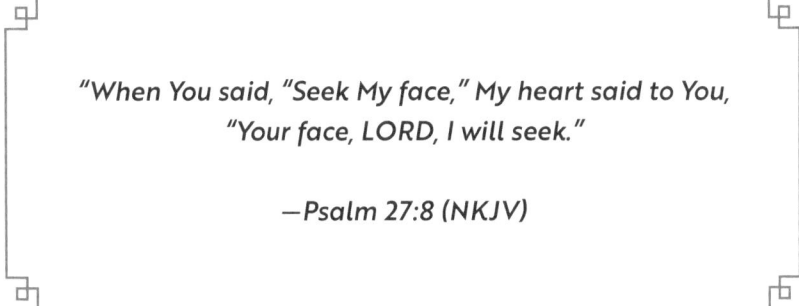

"When You said, "Seek My face," My heart said to You, "Your face, LORD, I will seek."

—Psalm 27:8 (NKJV)

A

WHY A JOURNAL

A journal is not a textbook, a "how-to" book, or academic study on theology. A journal is a diary of observations, discoveries, and experiences. It provides a safe place to process, capture feelings, prayers, and anything considered significant, valuable, and worth remembering. A journal invites recurring, regular interaction—and use of it WITH God can become wonderfully relational.

This journal is designed to be a simple tool that will help develop and guide a lifestyle of reading your Bible and meditating on scripture more deeply and consistently. This journal's goal is to help the reader learn how to better know God, Jesus, and the Holy Spirit in a beautifully intimate and personal way.

WHERE TO START

Getting started is simple—start reading God's Word!

After years of not seeking Him, life was no longer as satisfying. I understood what King Solomon meant when, in all his wisdom and wealth, he was left empty and with a void in his heart that only God could fill. I was meandering, disconnected from Jesus, and knew the way back was through God's Word.

I could feel His relentless pursuit of me while laying in bed, filled with thoughts of deep regrets and falsely believing that He had let me down. Yet, the lies I'd come to believe were washed away by the truth of His Word. Verses I'd spent years not thinking about came like a flood, overwhelming my soul. With a heart to deconstruct and willingly challenge all that I had been taught, I heard His gentle whisper telling me to simply get to know Him. After many nights of saying, "No, I'm not going to give you my heart again," one night I picked up my Bible and just started reading.

To my amazement, the more I read His Word, the more I wanted. My hunger for Jesus grew and compounded. What I found was a gentle and lowly Savior who wanted to set me free from religiosity and showed me how deep and wide was His love for me—something I'd never truly understood.

Nowadays, I can't get enough of Him and His Word! My heart is full of joy, purpose, and passion to share with others what I've experienced through more deeply abiding in Him.

The Bible is the infallible Word of God. 2 Timothy 3:16-17 says that "all Scripture is given by inspiration of God." Hebrews 4:12 tells us "the word of God is living and active..., discerning the thoughts and intentions of the heart." And Psalm 138:2 makes it clear that our Sovereign God has "exalted" His Word "above all things." If God Himself exalts His Word, then surely we should hold it in high esteem and make reading it our greatest priority. Yet, reading alone isn't sufficient. We must believe what He says.

RELATIONSHIP

Be mindful not to approach the Bible only academically. It's true, learning to love God with our mind involves gaining knowledge about Him, but knowledge alone should never be a replacement for a relationship with Him. Remember His Words are living and the dominant way He speaks to us. Be sure to always approach the Bible relationally and be expectant for what He will say to you.

It's important to seek God with a pure heart and motive. When our thoughts are consumed with self, sin, and the ways of this world—it becomes very difficult to focus on Him. But be encouraged, the Holy Spirit is there to help us. We can ask God (daily) to cleanse and purify our heart that we might encounter

Him (Psalm 51:10). We must also learn to take our thoughts captive to Christ whenever our thought life is dark, distracted, or dominated by fear, doubt, and unbelief (2 Corinthians 10:3–5).

As you grow closer to God, you'll become more aware that He's present in every moment of your life. Ask the Holy Spirit to open your eyes to see His movement in and around you. As you spend time studying God's Word, praying, listening, and reflecting... remember the Holy Spirit is there to guide you. Invite Him in every step of the way! If you face thoughts of uncertainty, ask the Holy Spirit to show you the truth and trust He will bring greater understanding. He is faithful and will always honor your desire to know your Heavenly Father and Savior more deeply.

Finally, be sure to approach this journaling experience with an open, teachable heart and willingness to grow in your faith. If you miss a day, don't get discouraged or quit. Just dive back into where you left off and keep going! God is patient and always ready to receive us when we draw near to Him again. His love will never quit on you.

HOW TO USE

HOW TO USE

The journal highlights 30 verses. Choose a verse to meditate on and study to help you develop a consistent rhythm of reading scripture with intention. How long you meditate is up to you and the prompting of the Spirit. You'll see additional verses you can read to go deeper in your meditation, plus a responsive prayer to encourage your daily interaction with God as you read His Word. Before and during your readings, invite the Holy Spirit to illuminate whatever He wants to reveal, teach, or speak to you. Our God is alive and willing to communicate when we seek Him with all our heart (Jeremiah 29:13).

GO DEEPER

Context is everything! Grab your Bible, look up the verse, read the supporting verses to gain the full context and greater understanding. Be sure to journal what you discover, what God is showing you, and consider writing out your own personal prayers. You'll be amazed when you look back at your journal entries and realize how specific God has been in guiding, teaching, speaking, and revealing more of Himself in all areas of your life over time. Your faith and trust will grow as you realize He really is with you!

DIFFERENT BIBLE TRANSLATIONS

I've included four different translations of the Bible to help you grasp the fuller meaning and nuances of the verses. The Bible was originally a collection of writings in Hebrew, Greek, and Aramaic; therefore, translations can and will vary due to efforts made to express the original languages in English. However, you can feel confident the core message in context remains the same. Take time to read each translation provided. This will open you to a broader perspective and may even inspire further digging as you seek to more deeply understand the nuances of the language in your verse.

Remember, an important part of your journey of abiding is believing that the God who created the universe and became flesh to die for our sins has protected and preserved His Word throughout the decades. As our Sovereign God, He will never allow man to alter His words. It's vital to approach the Bible with trust and belief that it is true, reliable, and has stood the test of time as the most printed document in the world. No other written document rivals the Bible, so we can rest and rely on the miraculous gift of the Holy Scriptures given to us!

PAGES FOR JOURNALING

Begin now to establish a rhythm of journaling what God reveals to you in His Word through prayer and reflection. Blank pages have been provided to help you get started. Use this space like a diary where you can communicate your thoughts, emotions, even doubts and questions to God. Capture what you discover in scripture that's meaningful and speaks specifically to you. Journaling daily in a posture of prayer can become beautifully interactive with God. And as you express your prayers, realize they become a testimony of your faith and trust in God. Be patient as you wait for answers, and believe God's promise in Isaiah 55:11 that His Word will always accomplish what He purposes.

BIBLE READING PLAN:

On page 17, you'll find a New Testament (NT) reading plan. The order will differ from your Bible. I wanted you to read the witness accounts of the four synoptic gospels (Matthew, Mark, Luke,

John) alongside related scriptures in later books of the NT. This approach allows you to start each section with the life and words of Jesus. The goal is first to know Jesus and understand what the disciple witnessed during His time with them, which radically transformed their lives while with Him and after His resurrection. After that, see how later writings of the apostles shed new light on the words of the Savior and expanded His teachings.

The reading plan has no specific dates, allowing you to progress at your own pace. As you read, remember who the main character of this holy and precious book is—the Triune God. Engage with Him in prayer as you read. Invite the Holy Spirit to illuminate the scriptures and speak to you. If you're up for a challenge, consider reading three or more chapters each day and you'll complete the entire New Testament in less than 90 days! But don't feel pressured to rush. Far more important than speed is to grasp the fullness of what you're reading and to take time to journal.

ENCOURAGEMENT FOR THE JOURNEY

TIME & PLACE MATTER

Choose a comfortable quiet location in your home and ideal time of day to read your Bible and journal. Setting aside a consistent time and place that's free from distractions will be vital to the quality of your experience with the Lord. I've found mornings to be my sweet spot. The first thing I do after waking is make my coffee, grab my Bible, journal, and pen—close the door and dive into my reading. It's become so much more than a routine, but rather a special time with Jesus that I treasure.

MEDITATE & MEMORIZE

Reading to check off a spiritual task on your to-do list won't be helpful in connecting with God on a deeper level. I encourage you to slow down when you read and even read the verses multiple times, asking the Holy Spirit to provide understanding and personal application.

After that, it's time to "hide" the verse in your heart by memorizing it. Scripture is living and powerful and, when hidden in your heart, will purify and enable you to live a victorious life pleasing to the Lord (Psalm 119:11). A practical way to memorize scripture is to write the verse on an index card, then take the verse everywhere you go. Tape it to your bathroom mirror or the fridge, place it on the dashboard of your car, even make it your phone's screensaver. The more you see the verse, the more you can recite it and commit it to memory. Training your mind takes time and discipline, but the benefits are endless.

Need more inspiration? Read all of Psalm 119!

STAY THE COURSE

If you miss a day reading God's Word, don't get discouraged or quit. Pick up where you left off and ask the Holy Spirit to help you stay consistent and hungry for more. Remember it's not a task or academic pursuit. Approach the Bible relationally. As you abide in Christ (John 15), you'll discover the abundant life Jesus promises in John 10:10.

FELLOWSHIP

Invite a friend or maybe even your small group to join you! Jesus is truly all you need, but we were not created to do life alone. Jesus encourages us to grow and live out our spiritual lives with others. Inviting a friend or friends to join you on your spiritual journey is a great way to inspire others and create accountability for yourself. Time alone with Jesus is vital to abiding, but learning with others will also cause exponential growth and great joy.

GO DEEPER

There are many free resources available to help you go deeper in your study of God's Word. Two excellent sources are Blue Letter Bible (blueletterbible.org) and Bible Gateway (biblegateway.com). These sites will allow you to locate and explore the biblical meaning of words and verses in their original language along with many additional study tools, commentaries, and more. Consider yourself a student of the Bible. As you dedicate quality time to deeper study, you will grow in profound ways.

Are you ready to get started? Let's begin with a prayer—and let's go!

May the God of all comfort enlighten the eyes of your heart as you seek a deeper relationship with Him. May the truth of His word wash over you and set you free to stand firm in the knowledge of His unconditional love. Hidden and held under the shadow of His mighty wings as you step into His perfect will for your life. In Jesus's name, amen.

NEW TESTAMENT READING PLAN

THE AWAITED MESSIAH HAS COME
Matthew, Hebrews, and James

THE IMPORTANCE OF FAITH AND DISCIPLESHIP
Mark, 1 & 2 Peter, and Jude

CHRIST CAME FOR ALL
Apostle Luke's testimony and writings; and Apostle
Paul's ministry and letters: Luke , Acts, Romans–Philemon

JESUS IS THE SON OF GOD
John, 1, 2, & 3; John and Revelation.

New Testament
READING PLAN

MATTHEW

(1) (2) (3) (4) (5) (6) (7) (8)
(9) (10) (11) (12) (13) (14) (15) (16)
(17) (18) (19) (20) (21) (22) (23) (24)
(25) (26) (27) (28)

HEBREWS

(1) (2) (3) (4) (5) (6) (7) (8)
(9) (10) (11) (12) (13)

JAMES

(1) (2) (3) (4) (5)

MARK

(1) (2) (3) (4) (5) (6) (7) (8)
(9) (10) (11) (12) (13) (14) (15) (16)

1 PETER

(1) (2) (3) (4) (5)

2 PETER   ## JUDE

(1) (2) (3)   (1)

LUKE

(1) (2) (3) (4) (5) (6) (7) (8)
(9) (10) (11) (12) (13) (14) (15) (16)
(17) (18) (19) (20) (21) (22) (23) (24)

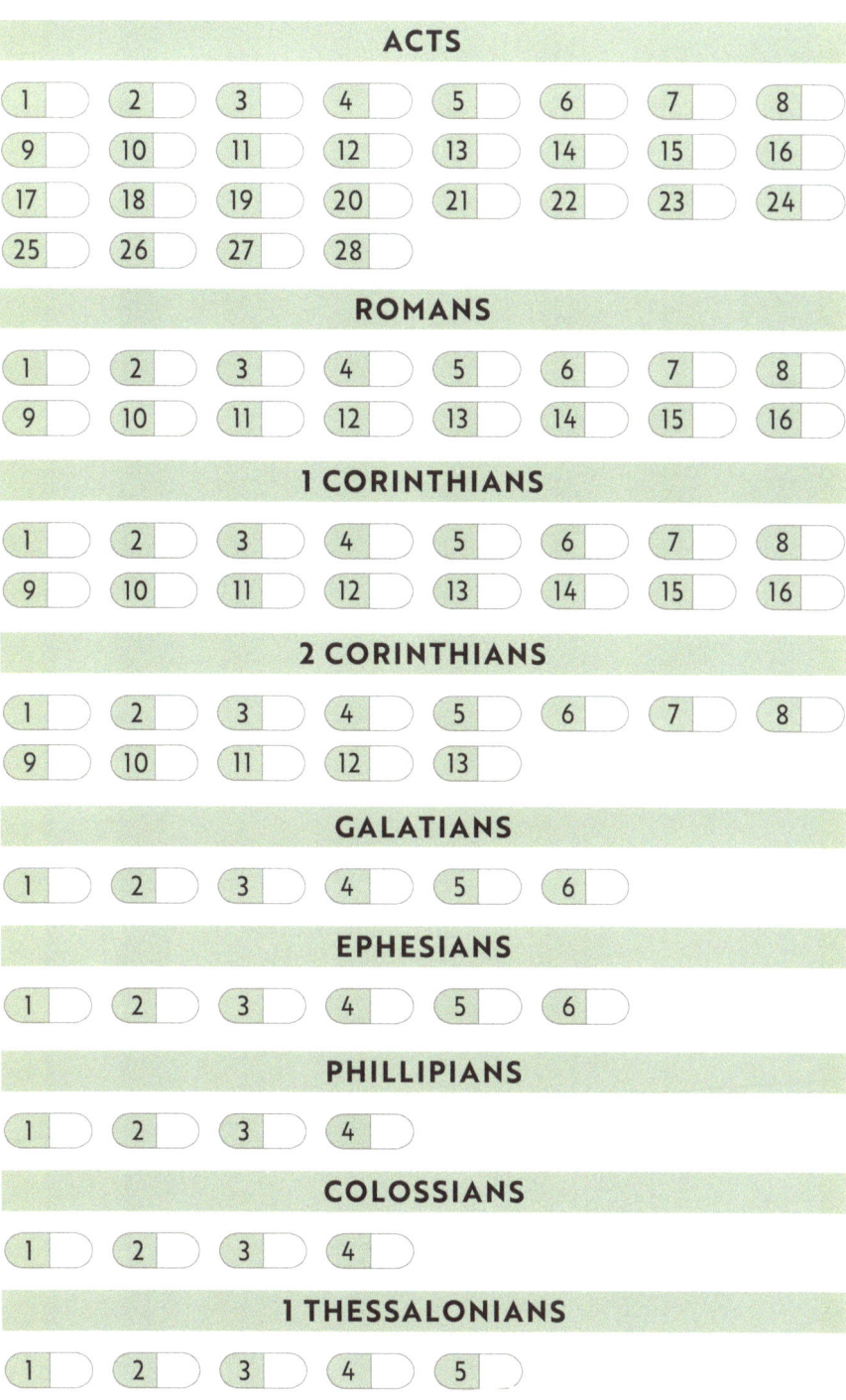

ACTS

1 2 3 4 5 6 7 8
9 10 11 12 13 14 15 16
17 18 19 20 21 22 23 24
25 26 27 28

ROMANS

1 2 3 4 5 6 7 8
9 10 11 12 13 14 15 16

1 CORINTHIANS

1 2 3 4 5 6 7 8
9 10 11 12 13 14 15 16

2 CORINTHIANS

1 2 3 4 5 6 7 8
9 10 11 12 13

GALATIANS

1 2 3 4 5 6

EPHESIANS

1 2 3 4 5 6

PHILLIPIANS

1 2 3 4

COLOSSIANS

1 2 3 4

1 THESSALONIANS

1 2 3 4 5

19

2 THESSALONIANS

1 2 3

1 TIMOTHY

1 2 3 4 5 6

2 TIMOTHY

1 2 3 4

TITUS	PHILEMON

1 2 3   1

JOHN

1 2 3 4 5 6 7 8
9 10 11 12 13 14 15 16
17 18 19 20 21

1 JOHN

1 2 3 4 5

2 JOHN

1

3 JOHN

1

REVELATION

1 2 3 4 5 6 7 8
9 10 11 12 13 14 15 16
17 18 19 20 21 22

DEVOTIONAL

WHY THESE VERSES

I was intentional on the selection of verses. Their focus is His abundant love and the great grace He has shown us. In order to fear and serve Him well, we first have to understand that the way He loves is not of this world. His love has no limits and is never contingent on our performance or acts of service. His love has the power to change us and purifies us from the inside out. The more our gaze is on Him, the less the problems of this world distract us and the better we can love those around us. I pray these verses move your heart to love God with all your heart, mind, soul, and strength so you may know how to love your neighbor as yourself.

WHAT TO EXPECT?

Throughout the Bible, we're told that if we seek God with all our heart, we will find Him (Jeremiah 29:13). We also learn in James 4:8 that if we draw near to God, He will draw near to us. Jesus even tells us that we, as Christ followers, are given the opportunity "to know the secrets of the kingdom of heaven" (Matthew 13:11). These are powerful invitations with powerful promises. And if we respond—IF we abide in Him and His Word—He WILL reveal more of Himself. Over time, you'll find more joy and more hunger for Him and the Spirit's movement in your life. You'll build a strong foundation for your faith, find freedom and passion for His mission, and begin to bear good fruit. Most importantly, you'll discover a beautiful intimacy with Christ that will overflow in your service to Him and all those around you.

A

Developing new ways of pursuing a deeper spiritual life takes time and effort, even sacrifice. But I promise if you'll take God's invitation to abide in Him and His Word, applying the insights you gain, it will change your life.

PS: I'll be doing this right alongside you and will be praying God shows Himself to you in beautiful, supernatural ways as you learn to abide in Him.

Are you ready to get started?
First, a prayer—and then let's go!

Father God, thank you for every person who is holding this journal in their hands. Thank you for their desire to draw closer and learn to abide more deeply in You. You see their step of faith and You are pleased. Holy Spirit, please enlighten the eyes of their heart and may the truth of God's Word wash over each one. As they seek to dwell more deeply in the scriptures, set them free to stand firm in the knowledge of Your unconditional love hidden under the shadow of the Almighty. Lead them step by step into Your perfect will for their life. Bless them and keep them forever close to You, in Jesus's name, amen.

Hebrews 4:12

FOR THE WORD OF GOD IS LIVING
AND ACTIVE AND FULL OF POWER
[MAKING IT OPERATIVE, ENERGIZING,
AND EFFECTIVE]. IT IS SHARPER THAN
ANY TWO-EDGED SWORD, PENETRATING
AS FAR AS THE DIVISION OF THE SOUL
AND SPIRIT [THE COMPLETENESS OF A
PERSON], AND OF BOTH JOINTS AND
MARROW [THE DEEPEST PARTS OF OUR
NATURE], EXPOSING AND JUDGING THE
VERY THOUGHTS AND INTENTIONS OF
THE HEART.

AMP

Hebrews 4:12 | DATE   M T W T F S S

NKJV

"For the word of God is living and powerful, and sharper than any two-edged sword, piercing even to the division of soul and spirit, and of joints and marrow, and is a discerner of the thoughts and intents of the heart."

ESV

"For the word of God is living and active, sharper than any two-edged sword, piercing to the division of soul and of spirit, of joints and of marrow, and discerning the thoughts and intentions of the heart."

NIV

"For the word of God is alive and active. Sharper than any double-edged sword, it penetrates even to dividing soul and spirit, joints and marrow; it judges the thoughts and attitudes of the heart."

GO DEEPER READING
Read Hebrews 3 and 4 ; Isaiah 55:11; Ephesians 6:17

PRAYER

Father, may Your word test my heart and reveal where any unbelief lies. You are faithful to reveal the depths of my heart. Please show me anything that needs to change. Unveil the root of my pain and heal me by Your word. You know my every thought and intention. Purify me. Thank You for always leading me in truth. In Jesus's name, amen.

JOURNALING YOUR REFLECTION

PRAYER

TESTIMONY

Matthew 6:33

BUT FIRST AND MOST IMPORTANTLY SEEK
(AIM AT, STRIVE AFTER) HIS KINGDOM AND
HIS RIGHTEOUSNESS [HIS WAY OF DOING
AND BEING RIGHT—THE ATTITUDE AND
CHARACTER OF GOD], AND ALL THESE
THINGS WILL BE GIVEN TO YOU ALSO.

AMP

NKJV

"But seek first the kingdom of God and His righteousness, and all these things shall be added to you."

ESV

"But seek first the kingdom of God and his righteousness, and all these things will be added to you."

NIV

"But seek first his kingdom and his righteousness, and all these things will be given to you as well."

GO DEEPER READING
Read Matthew 6:25-34; Matthew 5:6; 2 Corinthians 5:21; Philippians 3:9

PRAYER
Father God, please teach me to keep my eyes focused on You above all. Help me trust that You know every detail of my life and will provide all I need. You are a good and faithful Father. Show me Your glory so my faith will increase more and more. In Jesus's name, amen.

JOURNALING YOUR REFLECTION

PRAYER

TESTIMONY

John 15:15

I DO NOT CALL YOU SERVANTS ANY LONGER,
FOR THE SERVANT DOES NOT KNOW WHAT HIS
MASTER IS DOING; BUT I HAVE CALLED YOU
[MY] FRIENDS, BECAUSE I HAVE REVEALED TO
YOU EVERYTHING THAT I HAVE HEARD FROM
MY FATHER.

AMP

NKJV

"No longer do I call you servants, for a servant does not know what his master is doing; but I have called you friends, for all things that I heard from My Father I have made known to you."

ESV

"No longer do I call you servants, for the servant does not know what his master is doing; but I have called you friends, for all that I have heard from My Father I have made known to you."

NIV

"I no longer call you servants, because a servant does not know his master's business. Instead, I have called you friends, for everything that I learned from My Father I have made known to you."

 GO DEEPER READING
Read John 15:9-17; John 13:37-38; 1 John 3:16-24

PRAYER

Jesus, I remain amazed that You would actually call me Your friend! Thank You for revealing the heart of the Father and all He's made known to You with me. What an honor. Please help me be Your faithful friend by laying down my life, as You have done for me. In Your name, amen.

JOURNALING YOUR REFLECTION

PRAYER

TESTIMONY

Isaiah 26:3-4

"

YOU WILL KEEP IN PERFECT AND
CONSTANT PEACE THE ONE WHOSE MIND
IS STEADFAST [THAT IS, COMMITTED AND
FOCUSED ON YOU—IN BOTH INCLINATION
AND CHARACTER], BECAUSE HE TRUSTS
AND TAKES REFUGE IN YOU [WITH HOPE
AND CONFIDENT EXPECTATION]. TRUST
[CONFIDENTLY] IN THE LORD FOREVER
[HE IS YOUR FORTRESS, YOUR SHIELD,
YOUR BANNER], FOR THE LORD GOD IS
AN EVERLASTING ROCK [THE
ROCK OF AGES].

"

AMP

NKJV

"You will keep him in perfect peace, whose mind is stayed on You, because he trusts in You. Trust in the LORD forever, for in YAH, the LORD, is everlasting strength."

ESV

"You keep him in perfect peace whose mind is stayed on You, because he trusts in You. Trust in the LORD forever, for the LORD God is an everlasting rock."

NIV

"You will keep in perfect peace those whose minds are steadfast, because they trust in You. Trust in the LORD forever, for the LORD, the LORD Himself, is the Rock eternal."

GO DEEPER READING
Read Isaiah 25-26; Philippians 4:4-9

PRAYER

LORD God, please help me focus intently on You above all. Consume my mind with all Your goodness. No matter what challenges life brings, cause me to never lose sight of You and trust that You are in control. Thank You for being the Rock I can stand on securely. Thank You that when I set my mind on You, perfect peace comes. In Jesus's name, amen.

JOURNALING YOUR REFLECTION

PRAYER

TESTIMONY

1 John 4:4

"

LITTLE CHILDREN (BELIEVERS, DEAR ONES),
YOU ARE OF GOD AND YOU BELONG TO HIM
AND HAVE [ALREADY] OVERCOME THEM [THE
AGENTS OF THE ANTICHRIST]; BECAUSE HE
WHO IS IN YOU IS GREATER THAN HE (SATAN)
WHO IS IN THE WORLD [OF SINFUL
MANKIND].

"

AMP

NKJV

"You are of God, little children, and have overcome them, because He who is in you is greater than he who is in the world."

ESV

"Little children, you are from God and have overcome them, for he who is in you is greater than he who is in the world."

NIV

"You, dear children, are from God and have overcome them, because the one who is in you is greater than the one who is in the world."

GO DEEPER READING

Read 1 John 4; Romans 8:31; 1 John 5:4; Ephesians 6:12-13

PRAYER

Praise You LORD! Thank You for Your Spirit and Your power living in me. Without You, I know I'm vulnerable to the enemy. But with You alive in me, I can have confidence to overcome. Help me to always walk confidently knowing that You, the Creator of the universe, have my life in Your hands. In Jesus's name, amen.

JOURNALING YOUR REFLECTION

PRAYER

TESTIMONY

John 16:13

"

BUT WHEN HE, THE SPIRIT OF TRUTH, COMES,
HE WILL GUIDE YOU INTO ALL THE TRUTH
[FULL AND COMPLETE TRUTH]. FOR HE WILL
NOT SPEAK ON HIS OWN INITIATIVE, BUT HE
WILL SPEAK WHATEVER HE HEARS [FROM THE
FATHER—THE MESSAGE REGARDING THE SON],
AND HE WILL DISCLOSE TO YOU WHAT IS TO
COME [IN THE FUTURE].

"

AMP

John 16:13

NKJV

"However, when He, the Spirit of truth, has come, He will guide you into all truth; for He will not speak on His own authority, but whatever He hears He will speak; and He will tell you things to come."

ESV

"When the Spirit of truth comes, He will guide you into all the truth, for He will not speak on His own authority, but whatever He hears He will speak, and He will declare to you things that are to come."

NIV

"But when He, the Spirit of truth, comes, He will guide you into all the truth. He will not speak on His own; He will speak only what He hears, and He will tell you what is yet to come."

 GO DEEPER
Read John 16:5-15; John 7:16-18; 1 Corinthians 2:10-13

PRAYER

Jesus, thank You for not leaving me alone on the earth to find my way. Please Holy Spirit, forever lead me into all truth. Make me so sensitive to Your voice and Your guidance. Help me to listen more intently and respond to every word You share. I ask this in Your name, amen.

JOURNALING YOUR REFLECTION

PRAYER

TESTIMONY

2 Corinthians 3:18

"

AND WE ALL, WITH UNVEILED FACE,
CONTINUALLY SEEING AS IN A MIRROR
THE GLORY OF THE LORD, ARE
PROGRESSIVELY BEING TRANSFORMED
INTO HIS IMAGE FROM [ONE DEGREE
OF] GLORY TO [EVEN MORE] GLORY,
WHICH COMES FROM THE LORD,
[WHO IS] THE SPIRIT.

"

AMP

NKJV

"But we all, with unveiled face, beholding as in a mirror the glory of the Lord, are being transformed into the same image from glory to glory, just as by the Spirit of the Lord."

ESV

"And we all, with unveiled face, beholding the glory of the Lord, are being transformed into the same image from one degree of glory to another. For this comes from the Lord who is the Spirit."

NIV

"And we all, who with unveiled faces contemplate the Lord's glory, are being transformed into His image with ever-increasing glory, which comes from the Lord, who is the Spirit."

GO DEEPER READING

Read 2 Corinthians 3–4; 2 Corinthians 13:12; Colossians 3:10

PRAYER

Thank You, Lord God, that the veil has been lifted from my eyes. What an indescribable honor that I can now behold Your glory. Thank You that when I dwell in your Word, in worship and in Your presence—You transform me into Your likeness. I long to be more like You. Please help me draw nearer to You everyday. In Jesus's name, amen.

JOURNALING YOUR REFLECTION

PRAYER

TESTIMONY

2 Timothy 3:16-17

ALL SCRIPTURE IS GOD-BREATHED [GIVEN BY DIVINE INSPIRATION] AND IS PROFITABLE FOR INSTRUCTION, FOR CONVICTION [OF SIN], FOR CORRECTION [OF ERROR AND RESTORATION TO OBEDIENCE], FOR TRAINING IN RIGHTEOUSNESS [LEARNING TO LIVE IN CONFORMITY TO GOD'S WILL, BOTH PUBLICLY AND PRIVATELY—BEHAVING HONORABLY WITH PERSONAL INTEGRITY AND MORAL COURAGE]; SO THAT THE MAN OF GOD MAY BE COMPLETE AND PROFICIENT, OUTFITTED AND THOROUGHLY EQUIPPED FOR EVERY GOOD WORK.

AMP

2 Tim. 3:16-17 | DATE

NKJV

"All Scripture is given by inspiration of God, and is profitable for doctrine, for reproof, for correction, for instruction in righteousness, that the man of God may be complete, thoroughly equipped for every good work."

ESV

"All Scripture is breathed out by God and profitable for teaching, for reproof, for correction, and for training in righteousness, that the man of God may be complete, equipped for every good work."

NIV

"All Scripture is God-breathed and is useful for teaching, rebuking, correcting and training in righteousness, so that the servant of God may be thoroughly equipped for every good work."

GO DEEPER READING
Read 1 Timothy 3:13-17; Psalm 19:7-11; Romans 15:4; Psalm 119:9-11

PRAYER

Thank You, God, for the gift of Your Word that's powerful and purposeful to equip me for all the good works You've planned for my life. Help me to truly appreciate the value of the Scriptures and make reading them a daily priority. When I need wisdom and guidance, may I go to You and Your Word first. In Jesus's name, amen.

JOURNALING YOUR REFLECTION

PRAYER

TESTIMONY

Matthew 11:28-30

COME TO ME, ALL WHO ARE WEARY AND
HEAVILY BURDENED [BY RELIGIOUS RITU-
ALS THAT PROVIDE NO PEACE], AND I WILL
GIVE YOU REST [REFRESHING YOUR SOULS
WITH SALVATION]. TAKE MY YOKE UPON
YOU AND LEARN FROM ME [FOLLOWING
ME AS MY DISCIPLE], FOR I AM GENTLE
AND HUMBLE IN HEART, AND YOU WILL
FIND REST (RENEWAL, BLESSED QUIET)
FOR YOUR SOULS. FOR MY YOKE IS EASY
[TO BEAR] AND MY BURDEN IS LIGHT.

AMP

NKJV

"Come to Me, all you who labor and are heavy laden, and I will give you rest. Take My yoke upon you and learn from Me, for I am gentle and lowly in heart, and you will find rest for your souls. For My yoke is easy and My burden is light."

ESV

"Come to Me, all who labor and are heavy laden, and I will give you rest. Take My yoke upon you, and learn from Me, for I am gentle and lowly in heart, and you will find rest for your souls."

NIV

"Come to Me, all you who are weary and burdened, and I will give you rest. Take My yoke upon you and learn from Me, for I am gentle and humble in heart, and you will find rest for your souls. For My yoke is easy and My burden is light."

GO DEEPER READING

Read Matthew 11:25-30; John 6:37; Isaiah 11:10; Isaiah 61

PRAYER

Lord Jesus, sometimes I'm so exhausted and overwhelmed from all that life requires of me. Thank You for the invitation to come to You. Forgive me when I run to other sources, only to discover there's no relief. Please help me draw near to You and find true rest and peace. You are my Prince of Peace and I need You. In Your name, amen.

JOURNALING YOUR REFLECTION

PRAYER

TESTIMONY

2 Timothy 1:7

"

FOR GOD DID NOT GIVE US A SPIRIT
OF TIMIDITY OR COWARDICE OR FEAR,
BUT [HE HAS GIVEN US A SPIRIT] OF
POWER AND OF LOVE AND OF SOUND
JUDGMENT AND PERSONAL DISCIPLINE
[ABILITIES THAT RESULT IN A CALM,
WELL-BALANCED MIND AND
SELF-CONTROL].

"

AMP

NKJV

"For God has not given us a spirit of fear, but of power and love and of a sound mind."

ESV

"For God gave us a spirit not of fear but of power and love and self control."

NIV

"For the Spirit God gave us does not make us timid, but gives us power, love, and self discipline."

GO DEEPER READING
Read John 14:27; Romans 8:15; 1 John 4:18

PRAYER

Lord Jesus, thank You for giving me a spirit of power found in the authority of Your Name. Thank You for the unconditional love You alone bestow on me every day. I'm grateful You also give me a sound, disciplined mind that removes fear, doubt, and unbelief. Help me live by Your Spirit always. In Your name, amen.

JOURNALING YOUR REFLECTION

PRAYER

TESTIMONY

John 14:26-27

BUT THE HELPER (COMFORTER, ADVOCATE, INTERCESSOR—COUNSELOR, STRENGTHENER, STANDBY), THE HOLY SPIRIT, WHOM THE FATHER WILL SEND IN MY NAME [IN MY PLACE, TO REPRESENT ME AND ACT ON MY BEHALF], HE WILL TEACH YOU ALL THINGS. AND HE WILL HELP YOU REMEMBER EVERYTHING THAT I HAVE TOLD YOU. PEACE I LEAVE WITH YOU; MY [PERFECT] PEACE I GIVE TO YOU; NOT AS THE WORLD GIVES DO I GIVE TO YOU. DO NOT LET YOUR HEART BE TROUBLED, NOR LET IT BE AFRAID. [LET MY PERFECT PEACE CALM YOU IN EVERY CIRCUMSTANCE AND GIVE YOU COURAGE AND STRENGTH FOR EVERY CHALLENGE.]

AMP

NKJV

"But the Helper, the Holy Spirit, whom the Father will send in My name, He will teach you all things, and bring to your remembrance all things that I said to you. Peace I leave with you, My peace I give to you; not as the world gives do I give to you. Let not your heart be troubled, neither let it be afraid."

ESV

"But the Helper, the Holy Spirit, whom the Father will send in My name, He will teach you all things and bring to your remembrance all that I have said to you. Peace I leave with you; my peace I give to you. Not as the world gives do I give to you. Let not your hearts be troubled, neither let them be afraid."

NIV

"But the Advocate, the Holy Spirit, whom the Father will send in My name, will teach you all things and will remind you of everything I have said to you. Peace I leave with you; My peace I give you. I do not give to you as the world gives. Do not let your hearts be troubled and do not be afraid."

GO DEEPER READING
Read John 14; John 15:26; 1 John 2:24-29

PRAYER

Thank You, Father, for sending the Holy Spirit just for me—what a gift! I'm so grateful for a Helper, Teacher, and One who brings to remembrance the words of Jesus. Please help me to never quench the Spirit. And thank You Lord, that because of You, there is no fear...only peace. In Jesus's name, amen.

JOURNALING YOUR REFLECTION

PRAYER

TESTIMONY

.

Romans 5:3-5

AND NOT ONLY THIS, BUT [WITH JOY] LET US
EXULT IN OUR SUFFERINGS AND REJOICE IN OUR
HARDSHIPS, KNOWING THAT HARDSHIP
(DISTRESS, PRESSURE, TROUBLE) PRODUCES
PATIENT ENDURANCE; AND ENDURANCE, PROVEN
CHARACTER (SPIRITUAL MATURITY); AND PROVEN
CHARACTER, HOPE AND CONFIDENT ASSURANCE
[OF ETERNAL SALVATION]. SUCH HOPE [IN GOD'S
PROMISES] NEVER DISAPPOINTS US, BECAUSE
GOD'S LOVE HAS BEEN ABUNDANTLY POURED OUT
WITHIN OUR HEARTS THROUGH THE HOLY SPIRIT
WHO WAS GIVEN TO US.

AMP

NKJV
"And not only that, but we also glory in tribulations, knowing that tribulation produces perseverance; and perseverance, character; and character, hope. Now hope does not disappoint, because the love of God has been poured out in our hearts by the Holy Spirit who was given to us."

ESV
"Not only that, but we rejoice in our sufferings, knowing that suffering produces endurance, and endurance produces character, and character produces hope, and hope does not put us to shame, because God's love has been poured into our hearts through the Holy Spirit who has been given to us."

NIV
"Not only so, but we also glory in our sufferings, because we know that suffering produces perseverance; perseverance, character; and character, hope. And hope does not put us to shame, because God's love has been poured out into our hearts through the Holy Spirit, who has been given to us."

GO DEEPER READING
Read Romans 5; James 1:2-3; 2 Corinthians 12:9-10; Hebrews 12:10-11

PRAYER

Jesus, I don't like trials and suffering, but I'm grateful You use them all for my good. May I abide so deeply in You that I will always live with hope and even rejoice in my momentary suffering. Please, may Your love always overflow from my heart and life to all those around me. In Your name, amen.

JOURNALING YOUR REFLECTION

PRAYER

TESTIMONY

Proverbs 25:2

"

IT IS THE GLORY OF GOD TO
CONCEAL A MATTER, BUT THE
GLORY OF KINGS IS TO SEARCH
OUT A MATTER.

"

AMP

NKJV

"It is the glory of God to conceal a matter, but the glory of kings is to search out a matter."

ESV

"It is the glory of God to conceal things, but the glory of kings is to search things out."

NIV

"It is the glory of God to conceal a matter; to search out a matter is the glory of kings."

GO DEEPER READING

Read Proverbs 25; Proverbs 1:7; Isaiah 55:8-9; Romans 11:33; Psalm 19:1

PRAYER

Thank You, Father, for how deep and wide Your love is for me. There is so much in this Christian life that feels mysterious and concealed. But thank You for inviting Your people to search out spiritual matters. To search for You. Thank You that You promise I will always find You if I seek with all my heart. I'm seeking, Lord; please reveal more of Yourself to me. In Jesus's name, amen.

JOURNALING YOUR REFLECTION

PRAYER

TESTIMONY

Romans 12:2

AND DO NOT BE CONFORMED TO
THIS WORLD [ANY LONGER WITH ITS
SUPERFICIAL VALUES AND CUSTOMS], BUT
BE TRANSFORMED AND PROGRESSIVELY
CHANGED [AS YOU MATURE SPIRITUALLY]
BY THE RENEWING OF YOUR MIND
[FOCUSING ON GODLY VALUES AND
ETHICAL ATTITUDES], SO THAT YOU MAY
PROVE [FOR YOURSELVES] WHAT THE WILL
OF GOD IS, THAT WHICH IS GOOD AND
ACCEPTABLE AND PERFECT [IN HIS PLAN
AND PURPOSE FOR YOU].

AMP

NKJV

"And do not be conformed to this world, but be transformed by the renewing of your mind, that you may prove what is that good and acceptable and perfect will of God."

ESV

"Do not be conformed to this world, but be transformed by the renewal of your mind, that by testing you may discern what is the will of God, what is good and acceptable and perfect."

NIV

"Do not conform to the pattern of this world, but be transformed by the renewing of your mind. Then you will be able to test and approve what God's will is—His good, pleasing and perfect will."

GO DEEPER READING
Read Romans 12; Ephesians 4:22-24; Titus 3:5

PRAYER

Dear Lord, I pray for the mind of Christ. Please purify and transform the way I think and process and help me align every area of my life to Your will. Forgive me when I run after the world, even when I love it too much. Show me that Your ways will always be superior to the world's. Unveil my eyes so I can discover your perfect will for my life. In Jesus's name, amen.

JOURNALING YOUR REFLECTION

PRAYER

TESTIMONY

Romans 8:1-2

"

THEREFORE THERE IS NOW NO
CONDEMNATION [NO GUILTY VERDICT,
NO PUNISHMENT] FOR THOSE WHO
ARE IN CHRIST JESUS [WHO BELIEVE
IN HIM AS PERSONAL LORD AND SAV-
IOR]. FOR THE LAW OF THE SPIRIT OF
LIFE [WHICH IS] IN CHRIST JESUS [THE
LAW OF OUR NEW BEING] HAS SET YOU
FREE FROM THE LAW OF SIN AND
OF DEATH.

"

AMP

NKJV

"There is therefore now no condemnation to those who are in Christ Jesus, who do not walk according to the flesh, but according to the Spirit. For the law of the Spirit of life in Christ Jesus has made me free from the law of sin and death."

ESV

"There is therefore now no condemnation for those who are in Christ Jesus. For the law of the Spirit of life has set you free in Christ Jesus from the law of sin and death."

NIV

"Therefore, there is now no condemnation for those who are in Christ Jesus, because through Christ Jesus the law of the Spirit who gives life has set you free from the law of sin and death."

GO DEEPER READING

Read Romans 7 and 8; 2 Corinthians 5:17; John 5:24

PRAYER

Thank You, Jesus, for setting me free from sin and death! I will forever be grateful that in You, I'll never experience condemnation. Thank You for the gift of the Holy Spirit alive me. Please help me to abide in You and walk in the Spirit everyday. I love You, Lord. May my heart remain loyal forever. In Jesus's name, amen.

JOURNALING YOUR REFLECTION

PRAYER

TESTIMONY

Ephesians 1:17-19

"

[I ALWAYS PRAY] THAT THE GOD OF OUR LORD JESUS CHRIST, THE FATHER OF GLORY, MAY GRANT YOU A SPIRIT OF WISDOM AND OF REVELATION [THAT GIVES YOU A DEEP AND PERSONAL AND INTIMATE INSIGHT] INTO THE TRUE KNOWLEDGE OF HIM [FOR WE KNOW THE FATHER THROUGH THE SON]. AND [I PRAY] THAT THE EYES OF YOUR HEART [THE VERY CENTER AND CORE OF YOUR BEING] MAY BE ENLIGHTENED [FLOODED WITH LIGHT BY THE HOLY SPIRIT], SO THAT YOU WILL KNOW AND CHERISH THE HOPE [THE DIVINE GUARANTEE, THE CONFIDENT EXPECTATION] TO WHICH HE HAS CALLED YOU, THE RICHES OF HIS GLORIOUS INHERITANCE IN THE SAINTS (GOD'S PEOPLE), AND [SO THAT YOU WILL BEGIN TO KNOW] WHAT THE IMMEASURABLE AND UNLIMITED AND SURPASSING GREATNESS OF HIS [ACTIVE, SPIRITUAL] POWER IS IN US WHO BELIEVE. THESE ARE IN ACCORDANCE WITH THE WORKING OF HIS MIGHTY STRENGTH.

AMP

NKJV

"That the God of our Lord Jesus Christ, the Father of glory, may give you the spirit of wisdom and revelation in the knowledge of Him, the eyes of your understanding being enlightened; that you may know what is the hope of His calling, what are the riches of the glory of His inheritance in the saints, and what is the exceeding greatness of His power toward us who believe, according to the working of His mighty power"

ESV

"That the God of our Lord Jesus Christ, the Father of glory, may give you the Spirit of wisdom and revelation in the knowledge of Him, having the eyes of your hearts enlightened, that you may know what is the hope to which He has called you, what are the riches of His glorious inheritance in the saints, and what is the immeasurable greatness of His power toward us who believe, according to the working of His great might"

NIV

"I keep asking that the God of our Lord Jesus Christ, the glorious Father, may give you the Spirit of wisdom and revelation, so that you may know Him better. I pray that the eyes of your heart may be enlightened in order that you may know the hope to which He has called you, the riches of His glorious inheritance in His holy people, and His incomparably great power for us who believe. That power is the same as the mighty strength"

GO DEEPER READING

Read Ephesians 1; Isaiah 11:2; James 3:17-18

PRAYER

Oh Lord, how precious is the Spirit of wisdom and revelation you so freely give that I might know You better. Please enlighten the eyes of my heart more and more. I want to better understand the hope of Your calling, Your glorious inheritance, and Your great power toward me. Help me forever seek to know You more deeply and intimately. I love You, Lord. In Jesus's name, amen

JOURNALING YOUR REFLECTION

PRAYER

TESTIMONY

Galatians 5:22-23

BUT THE FRUIT OF THE SPIRIT [THE
RESULT OF HIS PRESENCE WITHIN
US] IS LOVE [UNSELFISH CONCERN
FOR OTHERS], JOY, [INNER] PEACE,
PATIENCE [NOT THE ABILITY TO
WAIT, BUT HOW WE ACT WHILE
WAITING], KINDNESS, GOODNESS,
FAITHFULNESS, GENTLENESS,
SELF-CONTROL. AGAINST SUCH
THINGS THERE IS NO LAW.

AMP

NKJV

"But the fruit of the Spirit is love, joy, peace, longsuffering, kindness, goodness, faithfulness, gentleness, self-control. Against such there is no law."

ESV

"But the fruit of the Spirit is love, joy, peace, patience, kindness, goodness, faithfulness, gentleness, self-control; against such things there is no law."

NIV

"But the fruit of the Spirit is love, joy, peace, forbearance, kindness, goodness, faithfulness, gentleness, and self-control. Against such things there is no law."

GO DEEPER READING

Read Galatians 5:16-26; Colossians 3:12-17; Psalm 1:3; Ephesians 5:9

PRAYER

Lord, please teach me to walk in the Spirit so I can cultivate and display the fruit of the Spirit. Open the eyes of my heart so I'm aware when my attitude and behavior doesn't represent Christ well. Make me especially sensitive to the Holy Spirit's movement in my life and help me draw closer so I might look more and more like Jesus. I want others to see You in me. In Your name, amen.

JOURNALING YOUR REFLECTION

PRAYER

TESTIMONY

2 Peter 1:5-7

"

FOR THIS VERY REASON, APPLYING YOUR DILIGENCE [TO THE DIVINE PROMISES, MAKE EVERY EFFORT] IN [EXERCISING] YOUR FAITH TO, DEVELOP MORAL EXCELLENCE, AND IN MORAL EXCELLENCE, KNOWLEDGE (INSIGHT, UNDERSTANDING), AND IN YOUR KNOWLEDGE, SELF-CONTROL, AND IN YOUR SELF-CONTROL, STEADFASTNESS, AND IN YOUR STEADFASTNESS, GODLINESS, AND IN YOUR GODLINESS, BROTHERLY AFFECTION, AND IN YOUR BROTHERLY AFFECTION, [DEVELOP CHRISTIAN] LOVE [THAT IS, LEARN TO UNSELFISHLY SEEK THE BEST FOR OTHERS AND TO DO THINGS FOR THEIR BENEFIT].

"

AMP

NKJV

"But also for this very reason, giving all diligence, add to your faith virtue, to virtue knowledge, to knowledge self-control, to self-control perseverance, to perseverance godliness, to godliness brotherly kindness, and to brotherly kindness love."

ESV

"For this very reason, make every effort to supplement your faith with virtue, and virtue with knowledge, and knowledge with self-control, and self-control with steadfastness, and steadfastness with godliness, and godliness with brotherly affection, and brotherly affection with love."

NIV

"For this very reason, make every effort to add to your faith goodness; and to goodness, knowledge; and to knowledge, self-control; and to self-control, perseverance; and to perseverance, godliness; and to godliness, mutual affection; and to mutual affection, love."

GO DEEPER READING

Read 2 Peter 1:1-11; Proverbs 4:23; Hebrews 11:6; Colossians 2:3

PRAYER

Lord Jesus, please teach me how to become more like You. I pray for Your divine power and motivation to diligently add to my faith more of Your character. Help me to study You and follow your example. And may I remain committed and disciplined to walk in Your ways and love others well. In Your name, amen.

JOURNALING YOUR REFLECTION

PRAYER

TESTIMONY

Jeremiah 33:3

"

CALL TO ME AND I WILL ANSWER
YOU, AND TELL YOU [AND EVEN
SHOW YOU] GREAT AND MIGHTY
THINGS, [THINGS WHICH HAVE BEEN
CONFINED AND HIDDEN], WHICH YOU
DO NOT KNOW AND UNDERSTAND
AND CANNOT DISTINGUISH.

"

AMP

NKJV

"Call to Me, and I will answer you, and show you great and mighty things, which you do not know."

ESV

"Call to Me and I will answer you, and will tell you great and hidden things that you have not known."

NIV

"Call to Me and I will answer you and tell you great and unsearchable things, which you do not know."

GO DEEPER READING

Read Jeremiah 33; Jeremiah 29:12; Psalm 91:15; 1 Corinthians 2:7-11

PRAYER

Oh Lord, I'm amazed that You are a living God who hears my prayers and answers! I'm so grateful Jesus made a way for me to live close to You. Thank You for this beautiful gift. Please reveal Your mysteries and mighty things to me. I long to know more of You and live a holy life before You. In Jesus's name, amen.

JOURNALING YOUR REFLECTION

PRAYER

TESTIMONY

Philippians 4:8

❝

FINALLY, BELIEVERS, WHATEVER IS TRUE, WHATEVER IS HONORABLE AND WORTHY OF RESPECT, WHATEVER IS RIGHT AND CONFIRMED BY GOD'S WORD, WHATEVER IS PURE AND WHOLESOME, WHATEVER IS LOVELY AND BRINGS PEACE, WHATEVER IS ADMIRABLE AND OF GOOD REPUTE; IF THERE IS ANY EXCELLENCE, IF THERE IS ANYTHING WORTHY OF PRAISE, THINK CONTINUALLY ON THESE THINGS [CENTER YOUR MIND ON THEM, AND IMPLANT THEM IN YOUR HEART].

❞

AMP

NKJV

"Finally, brethren, whatever things are true, whatever things are noble, whatever things are just, whatever things are pure, whatever things are lovely, whatever things are of good report, if there is any virtue and if there is anything praiseworthy—meditate on these things."

ESV

"Finally, brothers, whatever is true, whatever is honorable, whatever is just, whatever is pure, whatever is lovely, whatever is commendable, if there is any excellence, if there is anything worthy of praise, think about these things."

NIV

"Finally, brothers and sisters, whatever is true, whatever is noble, whatever is right, whatever is pure, whatever is lovely, whatever is admirable—if anything is excellent or praiseworthy—think about such things."

GO DEEPER READING

Read Philippians 4:4-9; Galatians 5:22; 1 John 3:3

PRAYER

Jesus, please deliver me from my anxious thoughts. Teach me to meditate on the goodness of who You are and the many blessings You give so freely. Destroy the lies I've believed and help me to dwell deeply on the truth of Your Word and Your character. In Your name, amen.

JOURNALING YOUR REFLECTION

PRAYER

TESTIMONY

Psalm 73:25-26

"

WHOM HAVE I IN HEAVEN [BUT YOU]?
AND BESIDES YOU, I DESIRE
NOTHING ON EARTH. MY FLESH AND
MY HEART MAY FAIL, BUT GOD IS THE
ROCK AND STRENGTH OF MY HEART
AND MY PORTION FOREVER.

"

AMP

NKJV

"Whom have I in heaven but You? And there is none upon earth that I desire besides You. My flesh and my heart fail; but God is the strength of my heart and my portion forever."

ESV

"Whom have I in heaven but You? And there is nothing on earth that I desire besides You. My flesh and my heart may fail, but God is the strength of my heart and my portion forever."

NIV

"Whom have I in heaven but You? And earth has nothing I desire besides You. My flesh and my heart may fail, but God is the strength of my heart and my portion forever."

GO DEEPER READING

Read Psalm 73; Psalm 23:1; Philippians 3:8; John 14:3

PRAYER

Lord, You are the only One who can satisfy the longings of my heart. Please move me to abide in Your presence even when things aren't the way I'd like them to be. Forgive me when I run to things I think will satisfy, only to discover I'm still empty. Please strengthen my heart. Thank You for being the "portion" I need. Help me desire You above all. In Your Name Jesus, Amen.

JOURNALING YOUR REFLECTION

PRAYER

TESTIMONY

Luke 17:20-21

"

NOW HAVING BEEN ASKED BY THE
PHARISEES WHEN THE KINGDOM OF GOD
WOULD COME, HE REPLIED, "THE KINGDOM
OF GOD IS NOT COMING WITH SIGNS TO BE
OBSERVED OR WITH A VISIBLE DISPLAY; NOR
WILL PEOPLE SAY, 'LOOK! HERE IT IS!' OR,
'THERE IT IS!' FOR THE KINGDOM OF GOD IS
AMONG YOU [BECAUSE OF MY PRESENCE].

"

AMP

NKJV

"Now when He was asked by the Pharisees when the kingdom of God would come, He answered them and said, "The kingdom of God does not come with observation; nor will they say 'See here!' or 'See there!' For indeed, the kingdom of God is within you."

ESV

"Being asked by the Pharisees when the kingdom of God would come, He answered them, "The kingdom of God is not coming in ways that can be observed, nor will they say, 'Look, here it is!' or 'There!' for behold, the kingdom of God is in the midst of you."

NIV

"Once, on being asked by the Pharisees when the kingdom of God would come, Jesus replied, "The coming of the kingdom of God is not something that can be observed, nor will people say, 'Here it is,' or 'There it is,' because the kingdom of God is in your midst."

GO DEEPER READING
Read Romans 14:17; Colossians 1:27

PRAYER

Jesus, thank You for clothing Yourself in flesh to bring the kingdom of God to earth so we might know You. I'm forever grateful You came to save us—to save me. Help me to live as a Kingdom citizen and shine Your light so others come to know You. In Your name, amen.

JOURNALING YOUR REFLECTION

PRAYER

TESTIMONY

1 John 4:1

"

BELOVED, DO NOT BELIEVE EVERY SPIR-
IT [SPEAKING THROUGH A SELF-PRO-
CLAIMED PROPHET], INSTEAD TEST
THE SPIRITS TO SEE WHETHER THEY
ARE FROM GOD,
BECAUSE MANY FALSE PROPHETS AND
TEACHERS HAVE GONE OUT INTO THE
WORLD.

"

AMP

NKJV

"Beloved, do not believe every spirit, but test the spirits, whether they are of God; because many false prophets have gone out into the world."

ESV

"Beloved, do not believe every spirit, but test the spirits to see whether they are from God, for many false prophets have gone out into the world."

NIV

"Dear friends, do not believe every spirit, but test the spirits to see whether they are from God, because many false prophets have gone out into the world."

 GO DEEPER READING

Read 1 John 4; Proverbs 14:15; 1 Thessalonians 5:21

PRAYER

Thank You, Lord, for Your Holy Spirit dwelling in me and able to discern all spirits. Please teach me how to evaluate every spiritual voice and influence against Your Word and Your character. Grant me the gift of wisdom and discernment so I'll know what is from You and what is not. You are the only voice I want speaking into my life. In Jesus's name, amen.

JOURNALING YOUR REFLECTION

PRAYER

TESTIMONY

James 3:17-18

"

BUT THE WISDOM FROM ABOVE IS FIRST
PURE [MORALLY AND SPIRITUALLY
UNDEFILED], THEN PEACE-LOVING
[COURTEOUS, CONSIDERATE], GENTLE,
REASONABLE [AND WILLING TO LISTEN], FULL
OF COMPASSION AND GOOD FRUITS. IT IS
UNWAVERING, WITHOUT [SELF-RIGHTEOUS]
HYPOCRISY [AND SELF-SERVING GUILE]. 18
AND THE SEED WHOSE FRUIT IS
RIGHTEOUSNESS (SPIRITUAL MATURITY) IS
SOWN IN PEACE BY THOSE WHO MAKE PEACE
[BY ACTIVELY ENCOURAGING GOODWILL
BETWEEN INDIVIDUALS].

"

AMP

NKJV

"But the wisdom that is from above is first pure, then peaceable, gentle, willing to yield, full of mercy and good fruits, without partiality and without hypocrisy. Now the fruit of righteousness is sown in peace by those who make peace."

ESV

"But the wisdom from above is first pure, then peaceable, gentle, open to reason, full of mercy and good fruits, impartial and sincere. And a harvest of righteousness is sown in peace by those who make peace."

NIV

"But the wisdom that comes from heaven is first of all pure; then peace-loving, considerate, submissive, full of mercy and good fruit, impartial and sincere. Peacemakers who sow in peace reap a harvest of righteousness."

GO DEEPER READING

Read James 3:13-28; Romans 12:9; 1 Corinthians 2:6-7

PRAYER

Father God, please fill me with wisdom from above—Your wisdom. May I be so hidden in You that my life displays all the beautiful attributes that come from abiding in You and Your wisdom. Help me to always make peace and yield my life to You. And may my life forever produce a harvest of righteousness. In Jesus's name, amen.

JOURNALING YOUR REFLECTION

PRAYER

TESTIMONY

James 1:5

"

IF ANY OF YOU LACKS WISDOM [TO GUIDE
HIM THROUGH A DECISION OR
CIRCUMSTANCE], HE IS TO ASK OF [OUR
BENEVOLENT] GOD, WHO GIVES TO
EVERYONE GENEROUSLY AND WITHOUT
REBUKE OR BLAME, AND IT WILL BE
GIVEN TO HIM.

"

AMP

NKJV

"If any of you lacks wisdom, let him ask of God, who gives to all liberally and without reproach, and it will be given to him."

ESV

"If any of you lacks wisdom, let him ask God, who gives generously to all without reproach, and it will be given him."

NIV

"If any of you lacks wisdom, you should ask God, who gives generously to all without finding fault, and it will be given to you."

GO DEEPER READING

Read James 1:2-8; Proverbs 2:3-6; 1 Kings 3:7-12; Jeremiah 29:12-13

PRAYER

Father God, so often I lack wisdom to make decisions or choose the right path in life. Thank You that you freely offer wisdom and invite me to just ask. So I'm asking, Lord—Please grant me wisdom to live in truth and walk along the best pathway for my life. I worship You, for You alone are all wise and all knowing. In Jesus's name, amen.

JOURNALING YOUR REFLECTION

PRAYER

TESTIMONY

John 15:4

REMAIN IN ME, AND I [WILL REMAIN] IN YOU. JUST AS NO BRANCH CAN BEAR FRUIT BY ITSELF WITHOUT REMAINING IN THE VINE, NEITHER CAN YOU [BEAR FRUIT, PRODUCING EVIDENCE OF YOUR FAITH] UNLESS YOU REMAIN IN ME.

AMP

NKJV

"Abide in Me, and I in you. As the branch cannot bear fruit of itself, unless it abides in the vine, neither can you, unless you abide in Me."

ESV

"Abide in Me, and I in you. As the branch cannot bear fruit by itself, unless it abides in the vine, neither can you, unless you abide in Me."

NIV

"Remain in Me, as I also remain in you. No branch can bear fruit by itself; it must remain in the vine. Neither can you bear fruit unless you remain in Me."

GO DEEPER READING

Read John 15:1-8; Galatians 2:20; Colossians 2:6; Romans 8:9-10; Ephesians 3:17; Jude 1:20-21

PRAYER

Lord Jesus, please forgive me when I live too independently and disconnected from You. I know without You, I can do nothing of significant value for Your kingdom. Help me stay close and deeply connected to You always. I ask this in Your name, amen.

JOURNALING YOUR REFLECTION

PRAYER

TESTIMONY

1 Samuel 16:7

"

BUT THE LORD SAID TO SAMUEL, 'DO
NOT LOOK AT HIS APPEARANCE OR AT
THE HEIGHT OF HIS STATURE, BECAUSE
I HAVE REJECTED HIM. FOR THE LORD
SEES NOT AS MAN SEES; FOR MAN
LOOKS AT THE OUTWARD APPEARANCE,
BUT THE LORD LOOKS AT THE HEART.'

"

AMP

NKJV

"But the LORD said to Samuel, "Do not look on his appearance or on the height of his stature, because I have rejected him. For the LORD sees not as man sees: man looks on the outward appearance, but the LORD looks on the heart.""

ESV

"But the LORD said to Samuel, "Do not look on his appearance or on the height of his stature, because I have rejected him. For the LORD sees not as man sees: man looks on the outward appearance, but the LORD looks on the heart.""

NIV

"But the LORD said to Samuel, "Do not consider his appearance or his height, for I have rejected him. The LORD does not look at the things people look at. People look at the outward appearance, but the LORD looks at the heart.""

GO DEEPER READING

Read 1 Samuel 16; 1 Peter 2:4; Hebrews 4:13; Psalm 147:10-11; Psalm 139:23-24

PRAYER

Father, thank You that you see beyond the exterior—You see the heart. You don't place value on what a person looks like. We've been made in Your image and You value each one of us. But You search the heart to see if we truly fear You. Lord, please create in me a clean and undivided heart that I may fear Your name. I ask this in the name of Jesus, amen.

JOURNALING YOUR REFLECTION

PRAYER

TESTIMONY

Ephesians 3:17-19

"

SO THAT CHRIST MAY DWELL IN YOUR HEARTS
THROUGH YOUR FAITH. AND MAY YOU, HAVING BEEN
[DEEPLY] ROOTED AND [SECURELY] GROUNDED IN
LOVE, BE FULLY CAPABLE OF COMPREHENDING WITH
ALL THE SAINTS (GOD'S PEOPLE) THE WIDTH AND
LENGTH AND HEIGHT AND DEPTH OF HIS LOVE
[FULLY EXPERIENCING THAT AMAZING, ENDLESS
LOVE]; AND [THAT YOU MAY COME] TO KNOW
[PRACTICALLY, THROUGH PERSONAL EXPERIENCE]
THE LOVE OF CHRIST WHICH FAR SURPASSES [MERE]
KNOWLEDGE [WITHOUT EXPERIENCE], THAT YOU MAY
BE FILLED UP [THROUGHOUT YOUR BEING] TO ALL
THE FULLNESS OF GOD [SO THAT YOU MAY HAVE THE
RICHEST EXPERIENCE OF GOD'S PRESENCE IN YOUR
LIVES, COMPLETELY FILLED AND FLOODED WITH GOD
HIMSELF].

AMP

NKJV

"that Christ may dwell in your hearts through faith; that you, being rooted and grounded in love, may be able to comprehend with all the saints what is the width and length and depth and height—to know the love of Christ which passes knowledge; that you may be filled with all the fullness of God."

ESV

"so that Christ may dwell in your hearts through faith— that you, being rooted and grounded in love, may have strength to comprehend with all the saints what is the breadth and length and height and depth, and to know the love of Christ that surpasses knowledge, that you may be filled with all the fullness of God."

NIV

"so that Christ may dwell in your hearts through faith. And I pray that you, being rooted and established in love, may have power, together with all the Lord's holy people, to grasp how wide and long and high and deep is the love of Christ, and to know this love that surpasses knowledge—that you may be filled to the measure of all the fullness of God."

GO DEEPER READING

Read Ephesians 3:8-21; Colossians 2:2-9; Revelation 3:20

PRAYER

Lord Jesus, please give me the ability to more fully understand and experience Your deep love. Teach me how to remain rooted and grounded in Your love—how to abide daily in You. And please fill me with all the fullness of God. With all my heart, thank You for Your love. There's no one like You. In Your name, amen.

JOURNALING YOUR REFLECTION

PRAYER

TESTIMONY

James 5:16

"

THEREFORE, CONFESS YOUR SINS TO ONE
ANOTHER [YOUR FALSE STEPS, YOUR
OFFENSES], AND PRAY FOR ONE
ANOTHER, THAT YOU MAY BE HEALED
AND RESTORED. THE HEARTFELT AND
PERSISTENT PRAYER OF A RIGHTEOUS
MAN (BELIEVER) CAN ACCOMPLISH MUCH
[WHEN PUT INTO ACTION AND MADE
EFFECTIVE BY GOD—IT IS DYNAMIC AND
CAN HAVE TREMENDOUS POWER].

"

AMP

NKJV

"Confess your trespasses to one another, and pray for one another, that you may be healed. The effective, fervent prayer of a righteous man avails much."

ESV

"Therefore, confess your sins to one another and pray for one another, that you may be healed. The prayer of a righteous person has great power as it is working."

NIV

"Therefore confess your sins to each other and pray for each other so that you may be healed. The prayer of a righteous person is powerful and effective."

GO DEEPER READING

Read James 5:13-18; Jeremiah 29:12-13; Psalm 34:15

PRAYER

Jesus, thank You for your promise that if I confess my sin, You will forgive. And for the gift of confession one to another that even brings healing. As I confess my heart, please bring revelation to all areas You want to heal in me and those I pray with. Thank You for Your great mercy. In Jesus's name, amen.

JOURNALING YOUR REFLECTION

PRAYER

TESTIMONY

Philippians 1:6

"

I AM CONVINCED AND CONFIDENT OF THIS VERY THING, THAT HE WHO HAS BEGUN A GOOD WORK IN YOU WILL [CONTINUE TO] PERFECT AND COMPLETE IT UNTIL THE DAY OF CHRIST JESUS [THE TIME OF HIS RETURN].

"

AMP

NKJV

"being confident of this very thing, that He who has begun a good work in you will complete it until the day of Jesus Christ."

ESV

"And I am sure of this, that He who began a good work in you will bring it to completion at the day of Jesus Christ."

NIV

"being confident of this, that He who began a good work in you will carry it on to completion until the day of Christ Jesus."

GO DEEPER READING

Read Philippians 1:3-11; 1 Thessalonians 5:23-24; Hebrews 13:20-21

PRAYER

Thank You, Lord, that You'll never give up on me. No matter how often I fail or fall short, You are working in me and promise to complete all You've begun in my life. I'm so grateful to be fully known and loved by You. You're truly a Good Father I can trust to sanctify me until I see you face to face. Thank You for this blessed assurance! In Jesus's name, amen.

JOURNALING YOUR REFLECTION

PRAYER

TESTIMONY

CLOSING THOUGHTS:

I was intentional on the selection of these verses, which focus on His abundant love and the great grace He has shown us. In order to fear and serve Him well, we first have to understand the way He loves is not of this world. His love has no limits, and is never contingent on our performance or acts of service. His love has the power to change us and purifies us from the inside out. The more our gaze is on Him, the less the problems of this world distract us and the better we can love those around us. I pray these verses have moved your heart to love God with all your heart, mind, soul, and strength so you may know how to love your neighbor as yourself.

WHERE TO GO FROM HERE?

Well done! You remained faithful to seek and abide in the Lord—and without a doubt, you've found Him. Now, hold on to Him. Spiritual growth does not happen overnight. It's a profound journey we have to choose to live out every day. Continue to seek and trust Him above all else. Be steadfast in your pursuit to go deeper with the only One who can satisfy your soul. Anchor yourself to His Word so that when the trials come you stand firm, because He who is in you is greater than he who is in the world (1 John 4:4).

Jesus shows us in the parable of the sower (Mark 4:1-20) that the condition of the soil is vital to bearing good fruit. The soil represents our hearts. If we're not careful, we can allow the cares of the world, the enemy, and even our own flesh to draw us away. Proverbs 4:23 instructs us to guard our heart so we will not be deceived. Be aware that "the enemy prowls around like a roaring lion seeking whom he might devour," (1 Peter 5:8) so we must make it our priority to abide in Him.

We are Christ's disciples. We are students who stay close and follow the steps of our Great Teacher, Jesus, who comes alongside and walks every step of the way with us. He, along with the Holy Spirit, will guide, correct, and support you (Luke 6:40). After His resurrection, some of the last words we have from Jesus are what's known as the "Great Commission" (Matthew 28:18-20). Here is where He calls us to take what we've learned about Him and teach all that He's commanded to others. Pray for boldness to share the love of Christ with others wherever you go.

Finally, if you close this journal and never open it again, I pray you will remember that abiding in Christ will be the highest goal from now until forever.

"Do your best to present yourself to God as one approved, a worker who has no need to be ashamed, rightly handling the word of truth." —2 Timothy 2:15 (ESV)

A